Guys, Shut Your Cakeholes and Listen!

How to Capture & Hold a Woman's Heart

Sean T. Taeschner, M.Ed.

authorHOUSE®

AuthorHouse™
1663 Liberty Drive
Bloomington, IN 47403
www.authorhouse.com
Phone: 1-800-839-8640

First published by AuthorHouse 03/10/2011

ISBN: 978-1-4567-4488-5 (sc)
ISBN: 978-1-4567-4489-2 (sc)

Library of Congress Control Number: 2011903987

Printed in the United States of America

Dedication

I dedicate this book to Araceli R. Andrada, the best female friend I have ever known.

A Society Dying of Loneliness

Hey, guys, one need only to turn on the evening news or log onto the Internet to discover that the world is falling apart when it comes to maintaining relationships. The causes for such breakups in relationships are many; however, the symptoms are as well. The greatest result of all of these issues causes loneliness for individuals. It is systemic and it is curable. This small book should help.

31 Days in Hell
(From Breakup to Wakeup)

From December 07, 2010 until January 08, 2011 I went through the worst breakup with my fiancé that I had ever experienced. I labeled the experience '31 Days in Hell' because of experiencing the separation from my loved one. It was as if God allowed me to experience part of a mini-judgment in which I got to see the pain I had caused others and was now to live for myself. I was a mess. I cried every other hour and felt depressed and lonely and angry at myself. Why did this happen to me? Was this breakup permanent? Had I wasted three years of my life for nothing in trying to work towards a marriage, only to have it all blow up in my face? Why? Would I awake from the nightmare I was experiencing? I had actually been in the meat department at Safeway gazing at fresh pork chops and lost it in front of my friend, Paul, who I was shopping with. "What's the matter, man?" He had asked. "Those pork chops remind me of the Pork Adobo she used to cook for me. I will never eat them again!" I bawled. It was embarrassing for Paul, as well as for me. I felt foolish.

Questioning my own actions I held out the hope that somehow the relationship might continue. We were not speaking by phone, e-mailing, or texting each other. In fact, in selfishness, we had each changed our passwords on our Facebook and Hotmail accounts. I put the cell phone in my own name. Neither of us sought to monitor the other's actions. IT WAS OVER. Would we allow ourselves to surrender foolish pride and wakeup? My twin brother began getting angry with me. We were roommates in the same apartment sharing food, utilities, and trying to feed our children post-divorce. His divorce had been recent. Mine had been 14 years earlier. "Stop your God damned crying. Suck it up, troop! Forget about her. Move on! Get back on the horse!" He was finding it difficult to watch me melt and suffer and not let go of her. He also hurt, because I was hurting so intensely. And, I knew in my heart, he had never truly fallen in love with a woman before. I had, and happy times were all that I had left to hold onto.

Feelings of suicide filled my head and I realized that, even though I had quit drinking four months prior to the breakup and was still dry, I felt like a failure and despair set in. I convinced myself that I would never hold her in my arms again nor feel her kiss on my lips.

Walking upstairs to where Paul had his apartment, I handed him my loaded Derringer, asking him to hold onto it for me indefinitely. I needed to keep trying to make up with my lost love.

Alcohol, Anger, and Abuse

Months before my breakup with the woman I love, I had come to the realization that drinking any type of drink with alcohol in it was not only bad for my insulin diabetes, but helped fuel deep angers within myself that I had never resolved. In stopping by our local church I asked for help and was received by a counselor who prayed with me. The desire to drink left me and I spent the next several weeks detoxing from being 'pickled' all of the time. I began gaining back lost weight and regained my appetite. I was beginning to heal.

In thinking about what caused me to fall apart I sat down to develop a picture for myself of what alcohol had done to me. The graphic below tells it all. I call it the Devil's Triangle.

Judging Others

In letting go of drinking alcohol I soon discovered how trapped I had been in my own selfishness towards others. I had been easy to judge others before judging myself. And, I had no right to do this. That was God's job, not mine. So, I stopped judging others by holding my tongue when I started to form an opinion of them. Believe me, it was difficult! Yet, I know that I would have been hurt by the same actions of others. My self-image needed improvement. Without using alcohol it was becoming easier to become the new me that others wanted to hang around and not run from.

I decided to write down more strategic ideas for ending such selfishness and addictive behaviors. I was going to become a man who would attract women and not be repulsive to them.

Therefore, this small book became the manual of strategic ideas for men to be used for capturing a woman's heart and holding it.

Drinking, Drugging, & Running

Are you a wild boy? Is the concept of preserving wildlife to you defined as throwing a party? Are your days of drinking, drugging, and running from the law over yet? Have you grown up? Will a woman have to worry about whether or not you are gambling away the paycheck as soon as you get it? Will the cops be coming to seize the nest if you are compromising it by doing drugs? What about her feelings and needs? Are yours based on pain and selfishness?

Why can't you lower your pride and go get help? Why can't you make changes in your life for everyone around you?

A Man is Logic, A Woman is Emotion

In giving up drinking and in giving up my gun to a friend when I was in trouble, I dared to remain alive and to keep growing. That was logical. Being a man I used the strongest tool available in trying to get help for myself.

I used what made sense. I decided to choose to keep on living and surviving; to allow common sense to rule over my feelings and emotions as I fought to stay alive. The battle was love and the enemy was hate, non-forgiveness, and anger. None of those feelings and emotions was based on doing what makes sense in order to keep growing as a person. I made the choice as a man to keep living and to help my fiancéescape from those feelings that were not of love. I decided to e-mail her and hoped for a response, which I finally received on January 08, 2011. It was an honest letter to me about the things both she and I needed to change in order to continue in relationship, as well as the statement, "I have never loved a man so deeply in my whole life." Surrender became easy and instant. Love took over logic. I would never be the same unforgiving, arrogant, abusive jerk to a woman ever again. I learned to listen and place her first. I won her heart back.

Once Born, Men Know How to Fix the Car & the House?

The largest fallacy ever perpetrated on males in the history of the world comes from the following beliefs: Once a man is born, he automatically knows how to fix the car, and fix the house. That is Bolshevik. Men learn these skills by watching other men who allow them to learn to use tools on the job as volunteers or paid staff. Since men are natural providers and protectors, it makes sense that they learn the skills of nest building and protection of the eggs in the nest once they have found a mate. Do not ever let a person convince you that males are worthless if they do not know how to repair the car or repair the nest (house). If a woman expects a man to know these things, she is dead wrong. You are more than a wallet or a meal ticket or Mr. Goodwrench. If a woman vocalizes or writes this to a man, she is not marriage material.

A Woman's Place Is….? (Protecting the Nest)

Women exist to civilize men, fluff up the nest, and protect the nest from males who might poke a hole in it so that the eggs fall out and break. They appreciate the food brought home by the male and the physical protection to her eggs and nest from outside enemies. She does not want the male pooping in the nest or not paying attention at his post due to drunkenness, excessive gambling, smoking, drugging, football watching, or outright laziness, so that food is not provided or the eggs grow cold and die. This is part of a woman's role in society, regardless if she takes on a career or finds other hobbies. The eggs always come first, guys. You come second. Her place is in the nest, period!

What a Woman Needs versus What a Woman Wants

A woman's needs come first. "Needs" are food, gas for the car, heat, clothing, water, sewer, garbage collection, medicine, and a reliable car to drive. Hopefully, it will not look ugly, and neither will her clothes or her hair, which leads to "Wants."

A woman's "Wants" are those items or services that one does not need in order to physically survive. Once the bills are paid, the leftover money is either saved or used to cover what one wants. Hopefully, it is split into savings and then some luxuries, such as getting one's hair done.

If a woman decides that a male is threatening the nest, she will throw him out of the nest and turn him off. She does this in order to help the eggs and herself survive. Notice that I used the word "threat." Are you a luxury item to her or something to be needed for survival?

Does "I want you" translate to "I care for you?" Or, does "I need you" translate to "I am going to use you."????? A man wants to be cared for, not used. Are you goods and services to her, or are you someone she wants to care for? Listen to the vocabulary she uses in speech and in text.

Words Both Genders Never Forget (Corrosive Comments)

Psychologists are most aware of the long-term damage to relationships in the workplace and at home when men and women choose to make corrosive comments to others. Negative feelings that show a loss of personal control and lack of sound judgment lead people to despair and chaos. Managers at work are circuit breakers in the process of making sure that many types of personalities get along at the workplace.

A female manager that I had at Seafirst Bank in Seattle once took me aside and said the following to me. "Sean, if you are able to get along with people at work, you will also be able to get along with people at home." This advice was unwanted, yet accurate. I could not deny her wisdom nor my need to make changes in my life that might lead me into better relationships with people.

One divorce later I understood her words completely. I remembered the many times I said vicious things to my ex-wife and to others in my life. Such comments began within two weeks of living together PRIOR to marriage. I never stopped to think about my ex-wife's feelings or needs, only my own. I did not show her kindness or caring from males. And, it damaged both of us and our daughter. The comments were fueled by angers that I had not dealt with in regards to my parents and the lack of courage I had in trying to change myself instead of others.

Dragging Up the Past

In addition to making corrosive comments to females in my past, I also had to work on the bad habit of dragging up the past hurts I felt my ex-wife had committed in our relationship. In every argument or fight we had had together, I would remind her of the things she had done to me and never stopped to consider the wrongs I had committed against her. How could our relationship even hope to be repaired when I was not an example of working to repair the bad habits I had latched onto? How could she hope to fight back with the list of wrongs I kept reminding her of? In essence, I was a bully shoving her face into the dirt and showing her no mercy in allowing her to get up and even repent of the things I was accusing her of, imagined or realized. Why would a female want to remain with a male bully?

Cakeholes versus Earholes (Truly Listening)

My twin brother had been in the Army R.O.T.C. at Seattle University and was taught to be tough as a soldier. Some of the comments they had drilled into him sounded eerily familiar. "Shut your cake holes and listen, God damn it! I am in charge here! Suck it up, troop. Are you whiners, winners, or wieners? There is no time for namby-pamby bullshit here!" I smile when I hear him say it today. That indoctrination for soldiers in battle is such verbal jujitsu and feelingless. It is designed to allow humans to operate as feeling less machines in order to kill others physically and spiritually. It is all about control and domination and single-sided victory. "Phony bravery" might be the buzzword for such verbiage.

I realized that I had become this tough Army-guy image with women. Women were to shut up and listen and keep their comments to themselves. I was the leader! Was I, really? Or, was I hiding behind an image that I had adopted in order to avoid personal change?

In losing my fiancé to this type of behavior I opened my eyes and my ears to the bad habits I had latched onto as a male, and I knew that the fix to be allowed to develop had to become listening. Females in this country have been screaming the number-one pet peeve for years to males. "He never listens to me!" Divorce and breakups have become the norm. Male mouths have operated poorly while male ears have remained plugged. Self-image protection and fear of change for male egos (self) had become the toxic cause.

Do You Know Yourself, Really?

If a male's ego is toxic, no female will want to be in his presence. Like poisonous mushrooms, his heart is afloat with toxic waste, flowing into the lives of others. Does he really know who he is or where he is going? Why does he fear growth? How is it that he can spread love and peace, if he is neither? The question is, "Do I know myself, really?" A man cannot give love freely, if he does not have it to give unconditionally, and does not know himself. How can he give what he does not have?

So, You Have Captured Her Heart?

In finding the love within yourself, have you been able to share it with your love? Have you captured her heart? And, if you have, can you hold it? What will it take to keep the love burning within you, so that you are a lighthouse to her in all of the storms of life that you will face together?

Appreciating Her Honesty

Women that write or speak from the heart help to civilize men. In pointing out the flaws she sees in a man that need change, she is trying to bring him to perfection before God and in the eyes and ears of others. A man is her diamond being polished so that it might be displayed as her trophy of love, her victory shaped deep in fire and stronger than steel. Her honesty runs through a man like a sword or like a hot knife through butter. It sears wounds closed in order that healing might take place in a man. Why be afraid of a woman speaking the truth, which is God? She is trying to hold a man accountable, which in the final judgment before God, a man cannot escape from;those acts which he has committed, nor the ones he willingly turned his back on. A woman's honesty guides a man into being willing to change in order to be a better protector, provider, and lover. His children shall follow his example.

Financial Security versus Emotional Security

A woman wants a man to consider her needs first. This means that a man must be a good provider to her in making sure that she and the eggs are fed, protected from physical harm, and protected from financial harm. He must have a job and be willing to work the hours needed to pay the bills in order to keep her from worrying. This is the role that a man is born into in American society. To fail in this role as a man leads a woman into emotional hell. Worrying is emotionally insecure work for women and creates fear, panic, mistrust, and a sense that the man is not meeting the family's needs. She then sees a boy instead of a man. She begins to feel like a surrogate mother, a role she never signed up for when she agreed to make a new life with him away from his own mother. Therefore, she may have to trade him in for a real man who can provide for her needs. When a man places her needs ahead of his, he is truly being the knight in shining armor sacrificing himself for the whole group. He is the hero falling on his sword. He is no longer a boy.

Building Her Up, Not Tearing Her Down

When men get angry they say things to women that are hurtful and never forgotten. Instead of allowing gentleness and love to guide his words, he allows despair and frustration to lead him into sarcasm and bullying behavior. He seeks to blame the woman for his shortcomings instead of seeing his problems through her eyes and ears. That is selfishness and does not build relationship nor trust. In order to build a trusting relationship with a woman, a man must be able to allow himself to build her up using kind deeds and words. A woman wants a man who will walk the walk, not talk the talk. She will remember the deeds as promises made, not promises broken. Are you a man of your word? Are you a man of action? Can you be trusted to keep your word once it has been released in trust to a woman? Look in the mirror for the answer. She is waiting.

Saying, Then Writing Thank You! (Appreciation)

A woman wants the entire man. She wants his verbal yes, as well as his written yes. In other words, tell her you appreciate her and then follow it up with a nice deed. Mail her a thank you card. Don't just give it to her. Go through the extra effort of addressing it, placing postage on it, and mailing it to her. Women love to be chased by men. This is one way to show her you still want to chase her. It shows her that you WANT her. And, if you can make the card, rather than buying it, it shows her extra effort on your part. Make it happen.

Putting Her First, Kids Second

Yes, you know that the children are important and usually the focus in your relationship. However, a woman needs to hear and see that a man considers her needs first. If a man places his children ahead of her, jealousy usually takes over and a woman feels that a man does not think she is important. It devalues or discounts her in the role of his lover, confidant, and friend. She actually wants you to be her best male friend first, then lover, second. If you had not made love with the woman first, the kids would never have arrived on the earth. She was first in line. Yes, they are important, yet they are the result of your having placed her in your life first. Children will see how you place their mother first, and then do it for the loves in their lives in the future. Remembering anniversaries, birthdates, holidays, and important milestones in her life will tell you that the trail of events that made her for you as her lover, are indeed an important road map to your following her through life. Again, it is all about being chased, guys, not just being chaste (pardon the pun).

Finding Out Her Pet Peeves (Pets, Guns, the House, & Shopping)

Most women fear men creating a dirty nest for its occupants. The nest becomes her trophy to other women that she is a successful lover to you and a mother to the children. It shows civility, order, and success in her life and those she cares for. For a man to allow pets to sleep in bed or poop on the floor or tear up the furniture and doors, shows his inconsideration of her feelings. Had you sat her down to ask her if you could both bring a pet into your lives? Will she be willing to feed and pamper it when you are working late and cannot come home? What about guns? Have you kept the ammunition locked up separately from the guns in a safe so that the children do not find them and decide to play with them and accidentally shoot themselves or others? Did you ask her about her feelings on the subject? Did you COMPROMISE or make declarations that neither of you could live with long term? Were you CONSIDERATE? When you go shopping with her, do you make a list of what is needed and then rush out of the store before she has had a chance to look for bargains in order to save the family money? Or, are you left staring at mannequins for hours while she looks for every item on the racks? Did you need to bring a book with you? Or, are you the guy who knows exactly what he needs from the store, goes in to buy it, then gets the hell out as fast as he can? Have you asked her why she needs to see every item in the store? Again, it is about conversation and compromise. She is not a mannequin. She is not plastic.

Arrogant Pride (Driving and Directions as Example)

Arrogance is known as 'boastful pride' and can be utilized by either gender. It is self-centered, non-caring, inconsiderate, and demeaning to others. In other words, it discounts a person by implying that another person is not as important as you are. When a man places his needs above a woman's, then she considers that he will be doing the same to her loved ones. Why would she be attracted to that?

A perfect example of this occurs with men and women daily. If a man is the driver and a woman is the passenger, she will most likely be the navigator with an open map and some common sense. A male will often say, "I know where we are going." He will turn off his ears to any suggestions by the female, such as, "We missed that left turn." The male will pretend he does not hear her and keep driving in the wrong direction. His pride is at stake. He will then get angry when he realizes that they are hopelessly lost and the female makes one more comment, which he will perceive as, "You fool, we are lost and you failed." The last thing a male ever wants to hear from a female is that he is a failure. Even if he knows she is correct, he will blame her for his having taken the wrong turn and discount her abilities as both a navigator and a driver. "Women drivers…they are all the same." Who is he really fooling? Why couldn't he listen to her suggestions? They might have made it to the party on time. Gentle men should never discount the suggestions of others. A gentle man will always admit when he is wrong and work to thank the person trying to help him. Women appreciate this kind surrender and will not rub a man's face into the dirt. Women are very merciful, guys. LISTEN!

Did You Have a Mother? (Hygiene, Dress, Bed sheets, Surrogate Mother, Being Her Trophy)

Women often state to each other, "I feel like I am raising another boy." Guys, why do you think that they make such statements? Do you think a woman really wants to replace your mother and clean up after you? Are you someone she wants to show off to her friends as her trophy, or someone she wants to hide from her girlfriends? Are you an embarrassment to her? What about your personal hygiene? How often do you wash your face, floss, shave, comb your hair, get a haircut, wear an ironed shirt, and have on clean underwear? Do you change your bedsheets every week or wait for her to do it? Do you wash the dishes, empty the garbage, sweep the floor, or wear house slippers…all without being asked? In other words, you may be a hero in her eyes as protector and provider. However, are you a bum? Do you wear the same clothes for days and rely on her to mend the holes in them, or do you mend them yourself? Why rely on her as your personal slave? Did you learn that habit while growing up or decide that women were slaves to men? It is all about your ATTITUDE towards females. How did you develop it? Is it healthy or corrosive in a relationship? Are you someone she really WANTS to be around and hold onto?

If you have learned poor habits, UNLEARN them! You will save your relationship from falling apart. After all, haven't you invested a lot of your feelings and emotions and finances into finding her? How about KEEPING her? If you can do it at home, you will be able to do it at work, too.

Asking Her Where the Landmines Might Be Then Checking (Background and Credit Checks, Transcripts)

Most men laugh when reading dating websites. Most female profiles state the same thing: WANTED: Man with a job; man with a (job) wallet; man who will spoon with me; man who will go for long walks on the beach; man who does not lie; man who does not cheat; man who won't make me his surrogate mother; man with recent pictures (not photos 10 years older than now). Have you ever seen this? WANTED: Boy with....

Are you laughing yet? Women are seeking a pedigree on a man. Why shouldn't a man be able to do the same with a woman? Remember the old joke circulating the Internet in which a father has his daughter's boyfriend complete an APPLICATION TO DATE MY DAUGHTER? The man is even polishing his shotgun. Hmm. Why?

Have you considered asking your potential female mate for life about her background? Have you asked her about her medical history? Is she on anti-depressants? Is she an illegal drug user or alcoholic? Did she graduate high school or college? Has she ever lived on her own? Did she ever do military service? What is her attitude towards gun ownership? What political party or religion does she like best? What were her grades like in school? Does she take people for granted? Has she spent time in jail? Does she pay her bills on time?

Are You Protector and Provider?

Men are genetically geared as physically strong. They are, by nature, protectors and providers to females and their children. This is both a genetic and spiritual role for men. When a man loses his job and cannot be sole breadwinner for the family, it does terrible damage to his psyche. This is especially apparent when the woman has the man stay home to watch the children as a Mr. Mom while she goes out to work and is bringing home a salary larger than what he had made when he was working. Why is this so difficult for males to understand? Why can't men be in the role of nurturer to children while a woman goes out to stress out on the job and have the heart attack first? (Just kidding). Our societal roles are driven by our fears of how others will judge us outside of our small family circle of trust. This is especially tough on women. Today's women are EXPECTED by other females to have the perfect hair, skin, fingernails, teeth, clothes, car, house, trophy husband, kids, and career. A man is expected to keep the home manicured outside, keep the home in good repair, keep the car in good repair, and keep a job. And, in the background, beyond survival mode, a woman is hoping that he will send her flowers, cards, and take her on exotic, unannounced vacations. Becoming too busy with survival leads to men forgetting a woman's needs beyond her EXPECTATIONS that a man will be there to physically protect her and bring home food and keep the bills paid so that she has no worries about the children's needs being met, too. Does this make sense, guys? Are you giggling yet? Does this stuff sound familiar to you? Will role reversal or helping understand a woman's needs really kill you as a male? Does it matter what your buddies think? Are they paying your bills for you? Does she see a man who is not only physically strong, but emotionally strong as well? Are you something to brag about to her friends? Think about it!

Understanding Her Culture and Yours

If you are a Caucasian male in America, this paragraph is for you. Most "white" males end up married to women from different cultures. This is a statistical fact and is very important when considering long-term relationships. Women that make comments regarding whether or not their mate truly knows them or not, goes deeper than just listening. Do you know her cultural background? Have you made the effort to learn her language, dress, foods, beliefs, customs, religion, or values? To make the effort to do so shows her that you, indeed, care for her. She will be looking for her father in you, as well as someone who will allow her to spread her culture to your children. Are you okay with that? Or, she may want to raise the children in your culture.

Have you asked her what her feelings are on this subject BEFORE you ask her to marry you? If not, why not?

It will be VERY important to her that you have even considered her feelings on the matter. Again, are you placing her first?

Does She Need You or Want You?

Men, again I ask you. Are you someone that she wants (cares for and loves) or someone she needs (a meal ticket)? FIND OUT! Watch what verbiage she uses and then ask her what she means by the words that were just used. It may surprise you. Then, discuss your feelings on the matter with her. Find out EARLY ON in the relationship. It may save you both from heartache in the end. Remember, the best relationships are maintained long-term as FRIENDSHIPS first. If she can brag about you to her female friends saying, "He is the best male friend I have ever had," then you will be her mate for life. Add loving and caring onto that and she will be yours to the grave and beyond.

Do You Need Her or Want Her?

Take what was read in the paragraph above and substitute the words he for she and she for he and think about it.

Is Woman Spare Ribs or a Soul-mate?

A woman is not the sum of all her parts. She is soul, too. God made her the ark to bring life into your life by wanting to have your babies. Is a woman more to you than just the spare ribs of Adam in the Creation Story in the Holy Bible? Is she a piece of sexual meat for your satisfaction and daily physical pleasures? Or, is she the female half of you that was a gift from God Almighty to you for life and into eternity? If you think that a woman is a piece of meat, then go rent one. And, if you are addicted to looking at pornography on the Internet or anyplace else, STOP doing it. Think about the greater harm you are causing to yourself, to her, your children, and to society. If you want to stop child sex trafficking, stop looking at porn!

Saying What She Needs and Wants to Hear

Here are but a few examples of statements I have used with the woman I love and call my soul-mate: I hear you; I am becoming a better man because of you; You are the best example of a woman to my children; You are pretty; You are elegant; I have always wanted this in my ideal dream of a female; God gifted you to me and I am happy to be your man; You complete me; Thank you for taking the risk to love me so completely with your heart and soul; I want to show you off to my buddies as my trophy and my wife; You are my greatest treasure.

Letting Her Know Your Dreams and Goals

Regardless of being married or not to the woman you love, have you shared your dreams and goals with her? Have you felt nervous about being the real you and letting your guard down and show her that you have hopes and want her to build towards them with her help? By eliciting or asking her for help, you are complimenting her, telling her that you completely trust her, and are building her up. You are showing trust and gentleness and exposing her to the man that will grow with her help, too. Women love that in a man. They also love it when a man focuses on raising his kids while at the same time, inviting her to help him. You are focusing on her needs and showing her kindness, caring, and gentleness. She will come running to you. You are her post.

Not Being Afraid to Be of Service

A gentleman not only opens the door for a lady, but he vocalizes and then shows his desire to serve her WILLINGLY. Guys, never be afraid to say to a woman, "May I be of service to you?" You are showing her that you can be a knight in shining armor and a gentle man as well. This is the Officer and a Gentleman role of "man in uniform" for a woman. Your armor is your willingness to protect her, then serve her. It is the moniker for the Los Angeles Police Department ("To Protect and to Serve").

Is This Your Dream or Hers, Really?

The biggest mistake I ever made in relationship with the woman I love, was to try to pressure her into marrying me. I had not considered her feelings and placed my dream of marriage on my schedule and said, "We are getting married at the courthouse next week!" Notice the exclamation mark in that last sentence? I was being DEMANDING like a drill sergeant. She was in MY army and I was in charge! What selfishness! I did not even realize that I was being so self-centered until I gave her a drop dead date to comply or I was going to end the relationship! Her letter to me regarding the matter was brutally honest and she gave me an out by stating to me that, "I have never been in love with a man so deeply before." I realized what a vicious fool I had been and begged for her forgiveness. Guys, don't be that God-damned stupid to females. Ask them what is in their plans and how it includes you. Do it gently. Let her know WHY you want to marry her and WHY it is on such a speedy timetable. Are you afraid of losing her to another man? Is she a procrastinator? Do you only have five months to live? Was she abused by males in previous relationships and just needs time to heal? Are you someone she wants to run after and catch or catch and release like a fish? How honest are you in communication with each other without trying to destroy one another's feelings? Did you ask her using kindness, gentleness, and caring? You decide!

Asking Her for Help

Women love it when men ask them for help. It shows them that you are not all talk, but rather all walk. It shows them that you can lower your pride and want to include them in the circle of trust that you have built for the two of you, and the kids if they exist. Remember, by tradition in marriage they are taking on your last name. Could that demonstrate to you that they want to live under the protection of your spiritual house? Are you allowing them to civilize you and the members of your collective home? I hope so.

Pictures in the Wallets and On the Walls

Women respect men that walk the walk and are not bull-shitters. Make sure to place their photos in your wallet and in your domicile and workshop. Place their photo on your desk at work. Remind them, yourself, and others that they are the most important person in your life and that God is at the center of your relationship. Include God's photo, too. Then, sit back and see what happens! Maybe she will reciprocate by your example. You are demonstrating what is important to you in public. She is your trophy.

Women Love the Chase and Making Up

Guys, do not be afraid to apologize to a woman that you love and then chase after her like you want to kiss her on the playground at recess. Women love it!

Truly Apologizing and Forgiving (Be the First to Reach Out)

Whether or not the fight was your fault or not, be the first of the two of you to show real strength and apologize and forgive if there has been a fight between the two of you. NEVER go to bed angry and let her know that the behavior was frustrating and not her person. Let her know that you still love her. BE a gentle man. Be considerate. BECOME caring and love.

Remembering the Little Things (Consideration and Appreciation)

The golden rule with women: In ALL WAYS, always remember her birthday, Christmas, Easter, anniversaries, holidays, funerals, and graduations with cards in the mail (hand-made are the best) and flowers. Women actually ache for guys to send them stuff. Other women feel envious of women that are being paid that much attention to. They, in turn, hope that the men in their lives were thinking of them so unconditionally and with such spontaneity.

Words to Songs with Deep Meaning

Make sure to try to e-mail your loved one daily. Include a romantic song from You-Tube as an attachment. This will show her that you are thinking of her EVERY day.

Women love it and will listen to the words of the songs over and over. Try it!

Becoming Her Heart and Holding It: My Promises (Vows)

I wrote the following vows (promises) to my fiancé.

January 10, 2011 http://www.youtube.com/ watch?v=_MaczkqNPBI

Dearest ***of My Heart, I Promise To You (My Vows):

- I promise to love you now and for the remainder of my life, and ask the same of you. I cherish you and want you. Because of you, I am becoming a better man, better father, and better person to others.

- I promise to keep growing. You have challenged me to grow beyond my selfishness. I love you for that. I promise to work my way out of selfishness while being your companion and lover.

- I promise to allow you to lead me back to God's true church. I promise to go with you when you invite me, no matter how far I must travel or how sleepy or lazy I have become.

- I promise to be gentle to you as a listener.

- I promise to stop judging you and to try to see things from your eyes and hear them from your ears first.

- I promise to not judge your family nor try to reorganize their way of thinking or try to change them. I will work, instead, on changing myself.

- I promise to thank God every day for the miracle of you in my life and thank him for having given you back to me to treasure.

- I promise to care for you as you grow older and become sick. I promise to be a caregiver to you and to accept whatever you need to stay alive.

- I promise not to judge you. Instead, I will look at myself and seek your wisdom and counsel.

- I promise to treasure your children and grandchildren; not take away their stuff, but help build them up spiritually, emotionally, and financially. They are your greatest work and masterpiece.

- I promise to protect you from those who will say bad things about you or try to harm you in any way.

- I promise to build you up, not tear you down.

- I promise to help you take care of your homes so that they might be available to you and your loved ones as an airport to land at in their brokenness...a safe harbor to heal at. The door shall always be open to them.

- I promise to share my food with your loved ones and give to them from my needs, not my wants.

- I promise to CARE for you, not use you in any way.

- I promise to wait until you are ready to do something...and not pressure you to do it.

- I promise to apologize to those I have hurt and seek their forgiveness. If I do not get it, I will let it go and accept the outcome and offer it up to God.

- I promise to show you mercy and forgiveness and patience when you are tired of life.

- I promise to change the things about myself that keep me from growing as a person.

I freely pledge my name and my children into your good care.

You are love to me and I do not EVER want to be separated from you again.

All my love,

Your Sean

Keeping God at the Center of the Relationship

A man is never too macho to be spiritual. He should never be afraid to let a woman know that he wantsto keep God at the center of the relationship. A man should invite his woman to church weekly and pray with her daily when waking up, eating, and going to bed. Showing her God's love by BECOMING God's love is being a real man. Try allowing Him to bless your relationship. In doing so, the real man will be an outward example to others.

Praying for Good Mates for Your Children

By including God at the center of your relationship, you are inviting Him to be the post for the two of you and your children. Then, pray to Him to provide good mates for your children's lives.

Remaining the Post (Becoming Gentleness, Kindness, & Caring)

Become the hitching post that your lady will want to tie her horse up to. Stand your spiritual ground by emptying yourself of the bad habits you might have developed and invite her to help you. In process, you will become gentles, kindness, and caring to her. Good luck.

Encouraging Others to Share Their Experiences

As a writer I believe that input from readers is vitally important to improving the product. This small book will see additional revisions in the future. I encourage those who have had similar life-changing experiences in relationships to write to me and give me written permission to publish their comments. I will only use first names, leaving out last names and cities. The form is below.

Date:

Name:

Address:

Phone:

E-mail:

Signature _

I give Sean T. Taeschner, M.Ed. permission to publish my comments in future editions of his book, ***Guys Shut Your Cakeholes & Listen! How to Capture & Hold a Woman's Heart.***

Any questions may be directed to me at: Trashner@ Hotmail.comor by writing to me at:

30708 229 PL SE; Black Diamond, WA 98010 USA (425) 301-3228